SCHIZOPHRENIA

Elaine Landau

Franklin Watts
A Division of Scholastic Inc.
New York • Toronto • London • Auckland • Sydney
Mexico City • New Delhi • Hong Kong
Danbury, Connecticut

Dedication

*For Dr. Carol Garmiza, a wonderful
psychologist and human being*

Cover design by John Gibson.
Interior design by Kathleen Santini.

Library of Congress Cataloging-in-Publication Data

Landau, Elaine.
 Schizophrenia / Elaine Landau.
  v. cm. — (Life balance)
Includes bibliographical references and index.
Contents: Schizophrenia—Schizophrenia: about the illness—
Schizophrenia: the symptoms—Schizophrenia: medication—
Schizophrenia: other kinds of help—Glossary.
  ISBN 0-531-12215-8 (lib. bdg.)   0-531-16614-7 (pbk.)
  1. Schizophrenia—Juvenile literature. [1. Schizophrenia.] I. Title.
II. Series.
  RC514.L295 2004
  616.89'8—dc22
                                    2003019775

Table of Contents

A Life-Changing
Illness

When eighteen-year-old Kelsey graduated from high school, her family couldn't have been prouder. She was awarded a full scholarship to a reputable college in Ohio where she planned to study music. Kelsey was considered her school's top violinist. She had been taking lessons since she was seven and one day hoped to play professionally in an orchestra.

Kelsey was looking forward to college in the fall, but the upcoming summer promised to be just as exciting. She and her best friend Sabrina had signed up for a special teen summer music program in the Berkshire Mountains of

Massachusetts. Kelsey had saved for nearly two years to attend the program, where she and Sabrina would have a chance to study with some outstanding musicians from the United States as well as abroad. Kelsey's entire family was at the bus station to see her off the day she left.

During the bus trip, however, Sabrina noticed that Kelsey was unusually quiet and withdrawn. Kelsey seemed different and stared out of the window for much of the ride. When Sabrina tried to tell her about a new piece of music she was working on, it was as if Kelsey hadn't heard her.

Things became even stranger when the bus stopped en route for its scheduled lunch break. Kelsey ordered a burger and fries but complained to Sabrina about the waiter. She said that he had been looking at her strangely and that she didn't trust him. Sabrina later remembered that Kelsey thought he was "up to no good." When Sabrina tried to contradict her, Kelsey became impatient and annoyed. Then, once the waiter brought Kelsey's food, she refused to eat it, insisting that it tasted "funny." Kelsey felt certain that the waiter had put something harmful in her food.

Sabrina didn't know what to make of all this but she just assumed that Kelsey was upset about being away from home for the first time. Sabrina ended up eating her friend's french fries and jokingly telling Kelsey, "You're crazy." It was a remark she would later regret.

The next few days were not what the girls had expected. They went to a concert together, but Kelsey ran out before it was over. When Sabrina tried to stop her, Kelsey angrily told her friend, "You stay away from me—you just stay away." After that unpleasant exchange, Kelsey ran all the way back to the dorm. Once she got there, she quickly packed her things and called her parents. She told them that she had to go away. Kelsey said that a man sitting behind her at the concert that night had put a gun to her head and had threatened to kill her. She thought that he had followed her back to the dorm and was probably lurking outside even at that moment.

Kelsey's parents told her to call the police immediately. Kelsey said that she couldn't because the man threatening her was one of "them." They asked to speak to Sabrina, but Kelsey claimed that Sabrina was in on the plot as well. Kelsey's call shocked and upset her parents. While they feared for their daughter's safety, they knew that something was terribly wrong. Kelsey sounded different, and the story she told seemed too incredible to be true. At that point in the conversation, Kelsey's father told her to stay where she was and that he and Kelsey's mother would be driving up to get her. Kelsey told them she couldn't wait; it was too risky to stay there any longer. With those words, Kelsey hung up the phone and left the dorm.

By the time her parents arrived, Kelsey was long gone. As it turned out, she had checked into a hotel to hide from the people she thought were after her. When she was found there nearly a week later, she hadn't left the hotel room once and the room was littered with half-filled pizza boxes and empty soda cans. The money Kelsey had saved for two years to attend the summer music program had been completely spent before she even had a chance to pay the program's registrar. However, that proved to be the least of her problems.

After her symptoms were evaluated and an extensive medical exam was conducted, Kelsey was diagnosed with a condition known as schizophrenia. It soon became clear that Kelsey's life would not be following the path she and her family had originally planned for her. They had to deal with the fact that Kelsey was now facing a serious mental illness.

A Breakdown in the Thinking Process

The National Institute of Mental Health describes schizophrenia as a chronic, severe, and disabling brain disease. Schizophrenia causes a breakdown in the thinking process. It's as if the mind of someone with schizophrenia has a short circuit, which causes it to continuously receive jumbled and confusing incoming signals. Schizophrenia affects the way people think, feel, and respond to those around them. As in

Kelsey's case, schizophrenia makes it difficult for the affected individual to know what is real and what is not.

> ### Not a Split Personality
> *The word "schizophrenia" comes from the Greek words schizo (split) and phrene (mind). That may be why some people think that schizophrenia means having a split personality, like the lead character in Robert Louis Stevenson's famous book,* Dr. Jekyll and Mr. Hyde. *In that story, Jekyll is a respected physician, while Hyde is a twisted murderer. The two men turn out to be the same person. This belief is one of many myths about schizophrenia, which is actually a disease characterized by a split from reality.*

Schizophrenia is not unique to the United States. It occurs in countries around the world. Schizophrenia affects people of all races, religions, and income levels. The National Institute of Mental Health notes that symptoms tend to appear in males in their late teens or early twenties. Though some females are affected in their teens, the disease most often surfaces in women in their twenties or early thirties.

A Costly Disease
Schizophrenia is among the most common mental illnesses in the United States. Approximately 2.5 million Americans

suffer from it. The National Schizophrenia Society cites that the illness costs the U.S. economy between $32.5 and $65 billion annually. This includes money spent on medical treatment, lost wages, and government supplementary-income payments to those affected.

> *"I live in a closet. Unlike most closets, mine is invisible. No one else can see it or touch it or even come inside to keep me company. Nevertheless, its imprisoning walls and terrifying darkness are very real."*
> *—Pamela*

Of course, anyone who has ever dealt with schizophrenia knows that there is a tremendous human cost as well. As Dr. Steven E. Hyman, former director of the National Institute of Mental Health, describes it,

> "Schizophrenia is particularly tragic because its onset usually occurs in the late teens or early 20s, just when families, society, and educational institutions have already put their full effort into launching a person into the world. Tragically, then we lose them, often to the chronic... inability to live up to their potential; often they withdraw from society and lose their ability to cope with everyday life."

Fortunately, the future for people with schizophrenia is brighter than anyone would have expected just a few decades ago. Today, there are new medications and other tools available to help people cope with the symptoms of the disease. While there is still no cure for schizophrenia, there is more reason to hope than ever before.

The Imprisoning Walls of Schizophrenia

Pamela's schizophrenia surfaced when she was a teenager. Although she earned good grades in high school, over time she found it more difficult to hide her problems. "I became virtually mute during the school day," she wrote in an article for *Schizophrenia Bulletin. "Because of this, and my habit of staring ahead even when addressed directly, some of the other students took to calling me 'the zombie.'" After receiving help, her mental health improved, and she is presently developing a career as a writer.*

Two

Determining the Cause

eah was a senior in college when she first started hearing voices. It was just before final exams, and she had spent a lot of time studying that week. One evening, Leah thought that she must have fallen asleep over her books when she suddenly felt as if she had been awakened by a voice telling her that her boyfriend was waiting for her at the mall and that she was supposed to meet him there. Leah had never made any such arrangements with her boyfriend, but at the time, she didn't feel quite sure of that. So she did what the voice said to do and went to the mall. After arriving, she looked in nearly every store and eatery, but her boyfriend was nowhere to be found. At the time, Leah brushed it off, thinking that maybe she had dreamed it.

Unfortunately, that wasn't the last time she heard that voice—or a number of other voices. There were visions, too. As a child, Leah had always loved stories about fairies. She adored those pretty, graceful, tiny creatures that rode on the backs of bumblebees or that danced on air. A fairly good artist, Leah also liked to draw fairies. The fairies she created had hair of gold and wore beautiful pink dresses made of sparkles. She always drew them with rainbow-colored transparent wings.

Now Leah began seeing fairies, but these were not like the others. She'd catch the outline of a fairy form as it flew away or see part of a wing as a fairy sat on her windowsill. Sometimes Leah thought she saw one making funny faces at her or momentarily flying across the television screen. In a strange way, the fairies made Leah feel powerful. At times, Leah thought that she was the fairy queen and ruled all of fairyland.

In contrast, the voices and visions that came to be part of the world of sixteen-year-old Eric were considerably darker. Eric often felt certain that someone was going to break into his room at night and kill him. The feelings became so terrifyingly real that he would move furniture and other objects in front of his bedroom door to keep out the intruder.

Eric also dangled hangers in front of his window, in case anyone tried to enter that way. He hoped that, if someone were trying to break in through the window, the clinking sound the hangers made would wake him and give him time to escape.

In addition, Eric was sure that someone was trying to poison him. Once, after his mother had given him a bowl of soup for lunch, he looked up at her and screamed, "Why did you put that poison in my soup?" As the days passed, Eric's fear grew increasingly intense. Finally, he decided that he could not trust anyone to prepare his meals, and he began to eat food directly out of the can. Most days, Eric lived in terror.

At the time, Leah's experiences were less threatening than Eric's. Yet, it turned out that both of these young people have schizophrenia, and both would have to deal with its impact on their lives.

A New Understanding

Today, most people understand that someone with schizophrenia is grappling with a serious mental illness. This has not always been the case. In prehistoric times, mental illnesses were not viewed as diseases. Instead, affected individuals were believed to be possessed by evil spirits, and an array of magical ceremonies were performed to cure them. In some cultures, holes were drilled into a person's head in an effort to drive out the evil spirits. Not many people survived this "cure."

During the Middle Ages, mentally ill people were often believed to be witches put on Earth to do the devil's work. Many of these individuals were burned at the stake, and others were drowned. By the 1600s, the situation had improved somewhat, but people still weren't sure what to do with mentally ill individuals who inhabited their towns and villages. Because people tended to feel uncomfortable around them, these affected individuals

Treatment Around the World

In most nations today, the mentally ill are cared for in hospitals or as outpatients in clinics or private medical facilities. Unfortunately, this is not the case everywhere. In some parts of the Ivory Coast, for example, people think that the mentally ill are possessed by evil spirits. Daily treatment often consists of being tied to trees, given small amounts of food, and beaten as well as prayed for. In some cases, villagers with schizophrenia have been treated this way for years. Mental-health organizations have tried to combat this sort of behavior on the Ivory Coast and elsewhere through education. However, much more needs to be done.

were often isolated. They were usually shut away with criminals and delinquents in penal institutions. There, mentally ill people were locked up in dimly lit, unheated dungeons where they remained chained to the wall. They were not given any type of medical treatment or even custodial care. There were no toilets, and these inmates were not bathed. Those who cried out too often or who simply annoyed their jailer were often beaten. Numerous mentally ill individuals spent years of their lives under such conditions.

It was not until the late 1880s that mental illness began to be seen for what it is—an illness—and was studied scientifically. In 1883, the German psychiatrist Emil Kraepelin started to identify specific mental illnesses; schizophrenia was among these. He labeled schizophrenia as an existing mental disorder, listing its symptoms and describing the course of the illness. This change of view was reflected to some degree in how the mentally ill were treated. Instead of shutting these people away, more attention was given to finding treatments and cures to control the problem.

Types of Schizophrenia

Over time, schizophrenia may progress through what are known as subtypes of the disease. Each subtype is

Dorothea Dix

In March 1841, a teacher named Dorothea Dix visited a Massachusetts jail, where she had volunteered to teach a bible studies class to female prisoners. When she arrived for her first lesson, she was surprised to discover a filthy, unheated facility in which the mentally ill were housed alongside hardened criminals. When Dix complained about the conditions, the officials in charge informed her that "the insane do not feel heat or cold."

Dix's experience compelled her to visit other facilities throughout the state, where she found similar conditions. Everywhere she went, she took notes on what she saw and interviewed the people she met. Dix compiled this data into a report that was eventually presented to the Massachusetts State Legislature. She lobbied for the passage of laws that would provide for the protection and care of the mentally ill. She also advocated housing the mentally ill in decent state-run facilities that would resemble hospitals more than prisons.

At the time, such ideas were unheard of and Dorothea Dix's suggestions were considered revolutionary. Mental illness was not seen as a treatable condition. People generally thought of the situation of the mentally ill as hopeless and believed that nothing could be done for them. Dix worked hard, however, to persuade people to see things in a more enlightened manner. She wasn't a medical expert, but she believed in the power of the human spirit and felt strongly that people could improve. Although it was an uphill battle, she eventually got the Massachusetts legislature to set aside money for special facilities for the mentally ill.

Dix did not stop with her home state. She set out to do the same work in other areas: She visited prisons and jails, and noted the conditions experienced by the mentally ill. She submitted reports to public officials and state governments with rewarding results. Thirty-two mental-health hospitals were eventually founded based on Dix's efforts, along with a number of similar institutions for the blind and the mentally retarded.

In her later years, Dix traveled throughout Europe, continuing her crusade to improve conditions for the mentally ill. She helped pioneer reforms in England, Scotland, France, Italy, Germany, Netherlands, Sweden, Belgium, and other countries. By the time she headed back to the United States in 1854, Dix had done much to improve the care and treatment of the mentally ill abroad.

Dorothea Dix is still best known for her work in the United States. She has earned a revered place in our nation's history and has been described as one of the most effective advocates of humanitarian reform during the nineteenth century.

characterized by a defining feature or behavior that occurs most often in that phase. As a result, one person may be diagnosed with various subtypes of the disease over a period of time.

According to the National Mental Health Association, different types of schizophrenia are:

- paranoid schizophrenia—this subtype is characterized by feelings of suspicion, persecution, or grandiosity (such as thinking that he or she is God), or a combination of these
- disorganized schizophrenia—this subtype centers on disorganization in a person's thought process; he or she is often incoherent in speech and thought but may not have delusions
- catatonic schizophrenia—a person who is diagnosed with this subtype often experiences disturbances in movement; he or she is withdrawn, mute, negative, and often assumes unusual body positions or facial expressions
- residual schizophrenia—a person with this subtype has no motivation or interest in life; he or she is no longer experiencing delusions or hallucinations
- schizoaffective disorder—this subtype features symptoms of both schizophrenia and a major mood disorder such as depression

Possible Causes for Schizophrenia

Today, researchers recognize schizophrenia as a medical illness. It has a biological basis, just like cancer or diabetes, only schizophrenia affects a person's brain rather than the body. Currently, it is believed that there is no single cause of schizophrenia. As with many other diseases, scientists suspect that several factors may be involved, among them genetics, prenatal factors, a chemical imbalance in the brain, and differences in brain structure.

Genetics

For years, scientists have realized that schizophrenia runs in families. People with a close relative who has schizophrenia are more likely to develop the illness. According to the National Institute of Mental Health, the identical twin of someone with schizophrenia has the greatest chance of developing it: The odds are as high as 40 percent to 50 percent. Someone with a parent with schizophrenia has a 10 percent chance of developing it. People with no family history of schizophrenia have only a one percent chance of getting the illness.

Recently, scientists have put a good deal of time and effort into studying the genetic factors of schizophrenia. Genes, or the units of hereditary information that are present in our cells, are passed down from parents to their offspring. Genes are a factor in much of what makes a person distinctive. Genes determine our eye and hair color as well as some of the medical problems we are prone to.

Some scientists suspect that multiple genes may be involved in predisposing someone to schizophrenia. After ten years of research, Professor Peter Falkai of Saarland University in Germany has helped to identify three genes that may play a role in schizophrenia. However, while three genes have been identified, Dr. Falkai has stressed that anywhere between fifty and one hundred genes could be involved in causing schizophrenia.

In a large study of adopted children in Denmark, it was shown that individuals who are biologically related to someone with schizophrenia are at a higher risk of developing the disorder. This was even true of adopted children who had never seen their parents or who had only limited contact with them.

> *"People do not cause schizophrenia; they merely blame each other for doing so."*
> *— Dr. E. Fuller Torrey*

Prenatal Factors

Some scientists think that what happens while a fetus develops in its mother's womb may have a bearing on whether that individual later develops schizophrenia. Factors that negatively affect a fetus's brain development may play a role. Studies have shown, for example, that mothers who had German measles or who suffered from malnutrition while pregnant were more likely to have children who developed schizophrenia. Recent studies done in Germany suggest that complications at birth or during pregnancy, as well as drug use during pregnancy, can have a similar effect.

The Father Factor

Though experts are not quite sure of the reason, a man's age when he fathers a child may be a factor in whether or not his child later develops schizophrenia. At age twenty-five, a man has a 1 in 198 chance of fathering a child who develops schizophrenia. As a man ages, however, the risk greatly increases. It doubles when a man reaches forty and triples for a man over fifty who fathers a child.

Chemical Imbalance in the Brain

People with schizophrenia may have a chemical imbalance in their brains. Some research indicates that they may produce too much of a substance called dopamine. Dopamine is a neurotransmitter, which is a substance that allows communication between the nerve cells that line the pathways of the brain. Neurotransmitters enable messages to be sent to different parts of the brain. In most people, the flow of

High-Tech Scans

Scientists know more about the brain's structure and function today because of high-tech scans such as magnetic resonance imaging, which was developed in the late 1970s, and functional magnetic resonance imaging, developed in the 1990s. These scans are usually performed in hospitals, large health-care complexes, or special MRI facilities. They are useful in diagnosing brain disorders because they provide clearer and more detailed images of the brain than other tools. Here's a closer look at what these scans do:

Magnetic Resonance Imaging
Magnetic resonance imaging (MRI) provides detailed images of the brain's internal structure. It can also be used to diagnose certain heart and blood-vessel diseases, cancer, and bone, joint, and muscle disorders along with other health problems. Using radio-wave pulses of energy, the MRI can zero in on a very small section of brain tissue. As it scans the brain's various sections, the data collected is translated into 2-D (two-dimensional) pictures. The information gathered can also be combined to create 3-D (three-dimensional) models. The MRI permits scientists to

study small parts of the brain and readily detect any structural abnormalities.

Functional Magnetic Resonance Imaging

Though it uses the same scanner equipment as the MRI, functional magnetic resonance imaging (fMRI) does not provide a view of the brain's structure. Instead, it offers researchers a picture of the brain's activity. This is accomplished by tracking the blood flow to the brain. As a researcher at the National Institute of Mental Health explains it, "The more active a brain area is the more blood flows to it. Thus, fMRI can provide a moment by moment movie of brain activity." Thanks to this new technique, studies using fMRI are beginning to shed light on mental illness.

Before having a scan, the patient is asked to remove all of his or her jewelry, keys, and other metal objects. The patient lies down on a table, which then slides into a machine that looks like an oversize cube. It's important to lie very still so that the pictures are clear. While inside the machine, which houses a magnet, the patient will hear a lot of clicks and humming sounds, but the entire scanning procedure is painless. A radiologist, a doctor who is trained to read scans, interprets the results.

dopamine is well controlled, but it is different for people with schizophrenia. They experience surges of dopamine, which disrupt the normal communication between cells and affect thinking.

Scientists are also exploring whether other neurotransmitters besides dopamine may be involved in the disease. "In the early 1990s the Dopamine Theory of schizophrenia was the primary focus for explaining what was happening with schizophrenia," explained Dr. Rajiv Tandon, an award-winning expert on the illness. "But the really interesting thing is that the current research is showing our explanation… for schizophrenia [along with the] prospects for future treatments don't need to be limited to the Dopamine Theory. There are other brain neurotransmitters that can also come into play in schizophrenia."

Differences in Brain Structure

In recent years, high-tech brain scans have allowed scientists to study both brain structure and function in greater detail than ever before. This has led some researchers to suspect that schizophrenia may be partly caused by a difference in the development of the brain. In numerous cases, the brains of schizophrenics have revealed some abnormalities. For example, fluid-filled cavities deep within the brain called ventricles have been shown to be enlarged while other regions of the brains of schizophrenics were decreased in size.

It is important to note, however, that not all the people with schizophrenia studied had these differences. In addition, similar differences sometimes appeared in the brains of people who did not have the disease. While these studies were conducted on living patients, researchers have also studied the brain tissue of people with schizophrenia following their deaths. In these cases, the brains of people who had died showed small changes in the number, structure, and location of some brain cells.

Though the cause of schizophrenia is still not entirely understood, researchers have been making steady progress in this area. It may be, in fact, that schizophrenia has several causes. Meanwhile, some things are certain. Schizophrenia is not caused by poverty or bad parenting. It is also not the fault of the ill person or the result of a personal failure on that individual's part. It is crucial that schizophrenia be seen for what it is—an illness. As psychiatrist Dr. E. Fuller Torrey once put it, "People do not cause schizophrenia; they merely blame each other for doing so."

Three
Understanding
Schizophrenia

"He's always been lazy and stupid," the voice from nowhere said. "You're right," a second voice agreed. "He'll never amount to anything. He's the lowest form of life on Earth. He's pond scum, a real mud crawler. He should have never been born. It's a waste of space on the planet."

Seventeen-year-old Mark sat in his high-school chemistry class listening in horror to this conversation about himself. It wasn't the first time; he had heard those voices before. Mark didn't realize that they were coming from inside his head. He was actually hearing this unflattering conversation as though two nasty people were sitting directly behind him.

Mark didn't know what to do when this happened at school. He wanted to run and hide. He wondered what his classmates and teachers would say after they heard what people really thought of him. Mark was sure that none of his classmates would ever want to sit next to him again.

But something amazed Mark even more: No one else ever seemed to hear the voices. From Mark's point of view, that was incredible. Those loud voices tormented him for days. They drowned everything else out. The voices seemed so real to Mark that he frequently found himself talking back to them, even shouting at them to go away and leave him alone.

The cruel voices began to interrupt Mark's life with increasing frequency. He couldn't think of anything else when he heard them. Worst of all, he had no control over the voices and was unable to make them stop. As it turned out, Mark would need professional help to do that. Soon after seeking help, Mark was diagnosed with schizophrenia.

The voices seemed so real to Mark that he frequently found himself talking back to them, even shouting at them to go away and leave him alone.

Symptoms of Schizophrenia

Schizophrenia affects people in different ways. No one can describe someone with schizophrenia and say that every person with this disease will experience it exactly the same way or have precisely the same symptoms. No single symptom can be used as an unfailing sign of the disease, and some of the symptoms people with schizophrenia experience can be found in other mental illnesses as well.

Before arriving at a diagnosis of schizophrenia, a doctor must take the patient's full medical history. The patient also has to undergo a physical exam and a variety of laboratory tests and scans to rule out other possible conditions. The patient may also be tested for commonly abused drugs. The body's reaction to those drugs is sometimes similar to the symptoms of schizophrenia.

At the core of schizophrenia is the person's inability to tell what is real and what is not. The most common characteristics of the disease are thought disorder, delusions, hallucinations, the feeling of being controlled by an outside force, and difficulty in expressing emotions.

Thought Disorder

Someone experiencing thought disorder, also known as disordered thinking, is unable to think clearly and sensibly. You might say that such a person is not "thinking straight." People with disordered thinking cannot focus their attention on one topic for long and are easily distracted. Thoughts or unrelated ideas seem to quickly dart in and out of their minds.

Trying to have a conversation with someone experiencing disordered thinking can be frustrating. The person may be hard to understand and may seem to be talking nonsense. For example, when asked his date of birth, one man with disordered thinking answered (all at once), "They pulled the oak tree out of the park; what's the matter with you—no dog likes spinach." Some people with disordered thinking tend to speak in meaningless rhymes. If you try to reason with someone in this state, it's unlikely that you'll succeed.

Delusions

Delusions, which are common in people with schizophrenia, are false, often bizarre, beliefs that the ill person holds. There are different types of delusions. Nearly one-third of people with schizophrenia suffer from paranoia, meaning that they feel persecuted by others. In some cases, these individuals may think that the CIA or the FBI is spying on them, or they may believe that their neighbor is trying to kill them with special rays that are invisible but deadly. One young man with schizophrenia believed that government agencies had planted transmitters and receivers in his apartment. "I could hear what they were saying and they could hear what I was saying. I also felt as if the government had bugged my clothing, so that whenever I went outside my apartment I felt like I was being pursued. I felt like I was being followed and watched twenty-four hours a day," he said.

It is not uncommon for people with schizophrenia to feel that there is a conspiracy against them. They may wrongfully believe they are being cheated, harassed, or threatened by others. Anyone can become part of the delusions, even close friends and family members who are actually trying to help the ill person. One young woman refused to continue sharing a bedroom with her younger sister because she thought that her sister would strangle her during the night.

Another young woman with schizophrenia believed that strangers who were watching her wanted to break into her house. "I thought I was being followed and my phone was being tapped," she said. "There was a hole in the ceiling of my closet, and I thought there was a wire up there. I thought they had installed microphones in my eyeglasses and [in] a dental filling."

Bob had a similar experience. Before being diagnosed with schizophrenia, he had a difficult senior year in high school. Bob firmly believed that the principal and guidance counselors at his school were plotting to keep him out of college. He later decided that they were also trying to kill him, so he would quickly turn and go the other way whenever he spotted one of them in the hall or outside the building.

"I felt as if the government had bugged my clothing, so that whenever I went outside my apartment I felt like I was being pursued."

The delusions of people with schizophrenia can take different forms. Some people with schizophrenia attach special meanings to everyday objects and events that only make sense to them. For example, they may believe that a television news anchor is talking about them or speaking directly to them through their television set. One young man with schizophrenia thought that an attractive woman who forecasted the weather was sending him messages through her dress color. Whenever she wore red, he thought that it meant that she loved him and wanted to spend the rest of her life with him.

Scott, a young man from a well-to-do family, was diagnosed with schizophrenia as a young adult. Scott had once been an outstanding student and athlete. Yet when he was about seventeen or eighteen, he noticed that things were becoming confusing for him and not making much sense. These symptoms continued to get worse as Scott became delusional.

When Scott went on a trip with a friend, he noticed how different he'd become. "The leaves in the wind seemed to be talking to me. Cloud formations had special meanings. Television and radio shows were talking about my life. And I thought that I could read people's minds and communicate with them without speaking." Scott also found what he thought was great spiritual meaning. "I truly thought that I had been blessed by God and that I had a direct pipeline to him. I felt happy and scared at the same time."

Hallucinations

People with schizophrenia are often plagued by vivid hallucinations. In a hallucination, the person sees, hears, feels, or even smells something that isn't there. There are many types of hallucinations, but most people with schizophrenia hear voices. The voices vary. They may sound like those of people the ill person knows or of people he or she is unfamiliar with. In some cases, people with schizophrenia carry on conversations with the voices. Other times, people hear several voices talking about them. Often, people with schizophrenia report that they've heard God and the devil arguing about them.

A researcher at the Royal College of Psychiatrists in London, England, describes what the voices are like:

"The voices can sound so real that you become convinced they truly are coming from outside you. It may be hard to work out why other people can't hear them. They may seem to be coming out of thin air, or you may hear them coming from the television or some other object. You may try to find an explanation for them—that they are coming from hidden microphones, loudspeakers, or the spirit world…. The voices are not imaginary but are created by our own minds. The brain mistakes our own thoughts for real experiences happening outside us."

Childhood Schizophrenia

Symptoms of schizophrenia are generally not seen in individuals younger than twelve years old, but they can occur that young in rare cases. The National Institute of Mental Health cites that childhood schizophrenia affects only about 1 in 40,000, compared to 1 in 100 adults. A researcher at the institute says that, "Parents may have reason for concern if a child 7 years or older often hears voices saying derogatory [unkind] things about him or her, or voices conversing with one another, talks to himself or herself, stares at scary things—snakes, spiders, shadows—that aren't really there, and shows no interest in friendships."

In children, the symptoms of schizophrenic psychosis (a mental state filled with hallucinations and delusions) tend to develop more slowly over a longer period of time. Sometimes, it starts with the child talking about strange fears that he or she feels are real. These children may cling excessively to their parents and speak about things only their parents understand. Some children become increasingly withdrawn and start to back away from others. They may seem to retreat into their own worlds.

In other cases, the disease does not appear until later, but the signs may be visible in childhood. According to the Harvard Mental Health Letter (a newsletter published by the Harvard Medical School), after viewing home movies, psychiatrists were sometimes able to identify children who later developed schizophrenia. These children differed from their brothers and sisters in several ways. The psychiatrists noted that they seemed somewhat clumsy, lacked warmth, and displayed odd head movements. Nevertheless, this is not true for everyone. Many people who develop schizophrenia show no such symptoms in early childhood.

Sometimes the voices heard by people with schizophrenia criticize or otherwise comment on a person's behavior and accomplishments. That's how it was for Carol North. Today, North is a respected psychiatrist conducting research at Washington University in St. Louis, Missouri. Yet things did not always go so smoothly for her.

When North was sixteen, she began hearing voices and was diagnosed with schizophrenia. "What's so cruel about these voices," North said, "is that they come from your own brain. They [the voices] know all your innermost secrets and the things that bother you most." The voices North heard belittled her school performance. "That was the horrible thing for me," North recalled. "The voices would say things like—'Carol North got an F' or 'She can't do it [get into medical school], she's not smart enough.'"

At times, the voices command the person with schizophrenia to do something. Some people have been told to steal items. Others have been commanded to commit suicide. People hearing the voices often feel they must do whatever the voices say, even if it means ending their own lives. The Schizophrenia Society of Canada reports that about 40 percent of people with schizophrenia attempt suicide, usually in an effort to escape the voices or the suffering caused by the voices.

Most serious violent acts by people with schizophrenia are directed toward themselves. Scott's brush with death came while he was traveling with his friend. He believed that God's voice told him to run his car off the road, which would bring him real peace and power in life. After doing so, of course, he found out otherwise. "I did this only to find no peace, just a totaled car and a trip to the state mental hospital."

Fortunately, Scott got help and is doing much better. Today, he is married, owns a thriving business, and feels at peace with himself.

The Feeling of Being Controlled by an Outside Force

People with schizophrenia may feel that their minds are being controlled by an outside force. Just as in science-fiction movies, where aliens from outer space invade and take over human bodies, people with schizophrenia may believe that a person, group, or unseen force is robbing them of their own thoughts and filling their minds with foreign ideas. According to a researcher at the Royal College of Psychiatrists, "It may get to the point where your whole personality seems under the influence of an alien force or spirit. This is a terrifying experience which people handle in different ways. In 'high-tech' societies, people tend to blame the radio, television, or laser beams, or believe someone has installed a computer chip in their brain."

Difficulty In Expressing Emotions

People with schizophrenia sometimes appear to have blunted, or flat, emotions. They may speak in a monotonous tone and display few facial expressions. Many of these individuals also tend to withdraw socially and to avoid contact with others. When placed in social situations, they often have nothing to say.

Some individuals with schizophrenia also lack motivation. They may not be interested in doing schoolwork or getting a job. Most lose interest in hobbies or activities they once enjoyed. In some cases, the person may not want to even get out of bed or leave the house. Their personal hygiene and housekeeping habits, such as washing their clothes, may also take a downward turn. During these periods, even the simplest things may seem like a great effort to the ill person. One person with schizophrenia describes these feelings by saying, "[I] couldn't take care of my hygiene; I couldn't wash myself or my clothes... I was not in control. Most of the time I had to sleep."

Dealing with the symptoms of schizophrenia on a daily basis can be difficult and challenging for anyone. People with schizophrenia do not get better on their own. They need the help of mental-health professionals and the support of those around them.

Violence and Schizophrenia

On December 7, 1993, during the evening rush hour on the Long Island Railroad, one commuter train was especially crowded. Every day, thousands of people in the New York metropolitan area take this commuter line to and from their jobs in New York City without incident. But that evening was different. A man named Colin Ferguson boarded the train in Jamaica, Queens, with a gun. After pushing his way to the middle of the car, he took out his weapon and began shooting. By the time he had finished, six passengers were dead and nineteen others were wounded. It's likely that his shooting spree would have continued if three men had not wrestled him to the floor while he reloaded his pistol.

It was later discovered that Ferguson had been previously diagnosed as having schizophrenia. While he was found sufficiently sane to stand trial, an insanity plea was his only real defense. Yet Ferguson, who was not thinking clearly, did not want that. He also refused to go along with the defense his attorneys devised. They hoped to argue that Colin Ferguson, a black man, had been so oppressed living in a racist white society that his mind snapped at the time of the

Violence and Schizophrenia
(Continued)

shooting. Ferguson fired the attorneys and insisted on representing himself.

Still delusional at the time of his trial, Ferguson's defense was that he was innocent and that someone had stolen his gun while he slept on the train. Even though dozens of eyewitnesses testified that he was the killer, Ferguson stuck to his story. He insisted that he was being framed for the murders and that another man was the real shooter. First, Ferguson claimed that a black man who had the same address he did was responsible for the crime. Later, he swore that the killer was white.

While Ferguson was examining witnesses, he occasionally made long speeches about how the police and prosecutors were conspiring against him. Ferguson also made a number of references to the bible, and he even compared himself to John the Baptist. When it was over, he was sentenced to six consecutive life sentences equaling nearly two hundred years of prison time.

The Colin Ferguson shooting made headlines across the country. It was obvious from his behavior on the train and at the trial that he suffered from a serious mental illness. Unfortunately, if a person with schizophrenia or other mental illness commits a horrific crime, the news and entertainment media often make it seem as if violence is a sure result of being mentally ill.

This is hardly the case. Most people with schizophrenia are not violent. To the contrary, many withdraw and prefer to be by themselves. A much greater number of violent crimes are committed by people who are not mentally ill. A researcher at the Schizophrenia Society of Canada explains that violence can occasionally result from mental illness if that person is not getting the right treatment.

It is important to remember, however, that such incidents are relatively rare. Ironically, although people often fear the mentally ill, these individuals are frequently taken advantage of and sometimes become victims of violence themselves. As noted earlier, people with schizophrenia have a higher suicide rate than the general population.

Four

Finding a Way Out

anice is a college graduate who has found success working in the editorial field. Things haven't always come easily to her, though. Janice has suffered from schizophrenia for more than twenty-five years, starting in her teens. "During my adolescence, I thought I was just strange. I was afraid all the time. I had my own fantasy world and spent many days lost in it. I had one particular friend; I called him the 'Controller.' He took on all my bad feelings… I could see him and hear him but no one else could."

Things did not get any better when she went off to college. "Suddenly, the Controller started demanding all my time and energy," Janice continued. "He would punish me if I did something he didn't like. He spent a lot of time yelling at me and making me feel wicked. I didn't know how to stop him from screaming at me and ruling my existence. It got to the point where I could not decipher [tell] reality from what the Controller was screaming. So I withdrew from society and reality."

"I couldn't tell anyone what was happening because I was so afraid of being labeled 'crazy.' I didn't understand what was going on in my head. I really thought that other 'normal' people had Controllers too."
—Janice

At that point, Janice was too out of touch with reality to get the help she needed. Yet help is available for people with schizophrenia. While there is no cure for schizophrenia, it can be treated. With treatment, individuals often begin to feel significantly better as well as function on a much higher level. A number of elements, such as medication, therapy, and support systems, go into a patient's treatment.

Drugs That Made a Difference

Medication is the most effective element of treatment. The drugs used to treat schizophrenia are known as antipsychotics. These medications help control some of the most distressing symptoms of the disease in many patients. For most people with schizophrenia, antipsychotic medications work to quiet the voices they hear as well as to stop the delusions. These drugs also help the user to "think straight" again. Antipsychotics have been around since the early 1950s. They allow people with schizophrenia to lead fuller lives.

The early antipsychotic medications, such as Thorazine or Haldol, which came out in the 1950s, reduced the action of the neurotransmitter dopamine. As noted earlier, people with schizophrenia experience surges of dopamine, which disrupt the normal communication between cells and affect thinking. These early medications, also known as neuroleptics, usually worked well to suppress (or stop) hallucinations, delusions, and disordered thinking. In some people, however, they had a number of unwanted side effects, including drowsiness, constipation, blurred vision, and abnormal involuntary body movements (muscle spasms, tremors, and slow, stiff movements).

While some of these side effects faded over time, some long-term users of these medications developed a condition known as tardive dyskinesia (TD). The most common symptom of TD is involuntary movements of the mouth, such as tongue rolling. In some cases, patients are not able to get their tongues back into their mouths. TD can also result in facial tics and jerky movements of the arms, legs, or neck.

The Newer Drugs

While such early drugs are helpful, they are not nearly as good as the medications available today. In seeking better ways to control schizophrenia, researchers developed new drugs. These are called "atypical antipsychotics," which appeared on the market in the 1990s. These drugs do not attempt to regulate dopamine alone but instead work on a broader range of neurotransmitters. The first drug of this kind is clozapine (brand name Clozaril). Clozapine worked for some patients for whom typical antipsychotic drugs were not effective. There were fewer side effects, as well.

However, clozapine is not free of problems. Some patients who take this drug tend to put on weight. Therefore, these individuals have to watch their diet and get plenty of exercise. One potentially dangerous side effect of clozapine is a serious blood disorder known as agranulocytosis. This condition involves a loss of white blood cells, which our bodies need to fight infection. Patients on clozapine must have a blood test every week or two to insure that their white blood cell count is within the normal range. Despite this inconvenience, clozapine continues to be prescribed for some patients for whom other drugs have not worked. Janice, the young woman described earlier, called clozapine her "true miracle drug" and claims to "have done remarkably well on this medication."

After clozapine, other atypical antipsychotic drugs were developed. These include risperidone (Risperdal), olanzapine (Zyprexa), quetiapine (Seroquel), and ziprasidone (Geodon). Unfortunately, all these drugs have some side effects. At times, such medications may cause fatigue, dizziness, weight gain, constipation, insomnia, and other symptoms. Some patients experience TD even on the new medications, but this is certainly less common. Overall, however, atypical antipsychotics are better tolerated by people with schizophrenia than the earlier class of drugs.

Timing Counts

Studies conducted by researchers at the University of California, Los Angeles, Neuropsychiatric Institute reveal that it is important to begin taking the medication prescribed for schizophrenia as soon as a diagnosis of the illness is reached. Research shows that the longer the symptoms remain untreated, the longer it will take to get the disease under control. In some cases, a long delay also lessens the person's chances for the best possible results.

People with schizophrenia who take antipsychotic medication vary in how quickly they improve. Some symptoms significantly lessen within days, while it can take weeks for even a small change to occur in other areas. If there is no substantial improvement, the patient's doctor will usually try another medication. In some cases, a doctor may have to prescribe several different drugs before the right one is found.

It is important that patients follow their doctors' directions and continue taking their pills even if they feel better. Many people with schizophrenia need to remain on their medication for an extended period to continue to feel well. At times, the medication is continued at as low a dosage as possible to control the illness's symptoms. This is known as maintenance treatment. The goal is to prevent the patient from relapsing into full-blown schizophrenia. It may also remove or reduce symptoms in others. Antipsychotic medications can be taken for months or even years because they are not addictive and patients do not become physically dependent on them.

While antipsychotic drugs have been helpful to large numbers of people with schizophrenia, they are not wonder drugs. Even individuals who take their medication regularly can have relapses even though they haven't skipped a pill. However, these episodes are usually less frequent and less intense than in people who decide to stop taking their medication on their own. Often during a relapse, the person's doctor prescribes a higher dose of the medication to prevent a full-blown return of the symptoms. In many cases this has been helpful in getting the ill person back on track.

Back on Track

Many people with schizophrenia feel that being given the right medication has changed their lives. Jeanie, a young woman who has struggled with schizophrenia for some time, is among them. Here's how she describes what happened to her:

When my first episode of schizophrenia occurred, I was twenty-one, a senior in college in Atlanta, Georgia. I was making good grades, serving as assistant vice president of my chapter in my sorority and president of the Spanish club, and very popular. Everything in my life was just perfect. I had a boyfriend whom I liked a lot, a part-time job tutoring Spanish, and was about to run for the Ms. Senior pageant.

All of a sudden, things weren't going so well. I began to lose control of my life and, most of all, myself. I couldn't concentrate on my schoolwork, I couldn't sleep, and when I did sleep, I had dreams about dying. I was afraid to go to class, imagined that people were talking about me, and on top of that I heard voices. I called my mother in Pittsburgh

Back on Track
(Continued)

and asked for her advice. She told me to move off campus into an apartment with my sister.

After I moved in with my sister, things got worse. I was afraid to go outside and when I looked out the window, it seemed that everyone outside was yelling "kill her, kill her"...Things continued to get worse. I imagined that I had a foul body odor and I sometimes took up to six showers a day. I recall going to the grocery store, and I imagined that people in the store were saying "Get saved. Jesus is the answer." Things worsened—I couldn't remember a thing. I had a notebook full of reminders telling me what to do on that particular day. I couldn't remember my schoolwork, and would study from 6:00 P.M. until 4:00 A.M., but never had the courage to go to class on the following day. I tried to tell my sister about it but she didn't understand. She suggested that I see a psychiatrist, but I was afraid to go out of the house to see him.

Jeanie's path to recovery was not easy. She attempted suicide once and was hospitalized at least twice, but in the end, things got better for her. After she was released from the hospital, she returned to Pittsburgh and became an outpatient at a clinic. It took her six months to recover.

After taking an antipsychotic drug for almost two years, Jeanie began to see results. "All of the symptoms seem to have vanished. I have my own apartment. I am back in college... president of my chapter of my sorority, and, above all, more confident and happier than I have ever been in my life." Today, when Jeanie reflects back on the pains of the past, she considers them to be a learning experience. She sees the future as a challenge. "My doctor once asked me what I think taking medicine means and I replied, 'not being sick.' Today I take my medicine daily, just as a person with high blood pressure or a diabetic does. It doesn't bother me. Today I am really free!"

The Key to Recovery

Continuing their medication helps keep many people with schizophrenia out of the hospital. Yet, some patients refuse to take their pills. Their illness stops them from helping themselves. In some cases, these patients don't believe that they are sick, and they think that their doctors are trying to hurt them.

Clarence, a twenty-four year old with schizophrenia, had improved with medication but refused to continue taking pills because he was sure his doctor was trying to poison him. Without the drug, his symptoms returned in full force. Clarence stopped going to work and stopped shaving and showering. He believed that his neighbors were in on his doctor's plot to kill him. Only after his parents had him hospitalized and put back on medication did he begin to see things clearly again.

E. Fuller Torrey is a well-respected psychiatrist who has conducted research on schizophrenia and has written a number of books on mental illness. He has a personal interest in the subject because his younger sister has schizophrenia. Torrey has long been concerned with the problem of mentally ill individuals refusing to take the medication they need.

To handle the problem, Torrey believes in resorting to legal means. He stresses that state laws in many areas make releases from mental hospitals dependent on patients successfully following their treatment plans—including the taking of prescribed drugs. Torrey feels that patients who refuse to do so should be forced to return to the hospital.

On March 5, 1997, Torrey testified in Washington, D.C., before the House Subcommittee on Housing and Community Opportunity. The focus of the hearing was to address the needs of the homeless. Many homeless individuals are suffering from schizophrenia and other serious mental disorders. If untreated, their illness frequently makes them unemployable, which, in turn, contributes to their being homeless.

"The quality of life for homeless individuals with a severe psychiatric illness is a national disgrace. Studies have found that 28 percent of them get some food from garbage cans and 9 percent use garbage cans as their primary food source."
—Dr. E. Fuller Torrey

At the hearing, Torrey said that studies have shown that about half of all people with severe psychiatric disorders do not understand that they are sick and need medication. "The part of the brain we use to understand our needs is the same part of the brain that is impaired in these psychiatric diseases," says Torrey. "The person is convinced that the CIA really *did* implant electrodes in his brain or that he really *is* the president of the United States and that Israeli agents are blocking his access to the White House. Such individuals will not take medication voluntarily because they do not believe that they are sick."

Not everyone agrees with Torrey on this issue. Lawyers from the American Civil Liberties Union (ACLU) have argued that forcing the mentally ill to take their medication violates patients' rights. These lawyers, along with many other individuals, think that the mentally ill should have a choice and should not be forced to swallow a pill they don't want to take. In response, Torrey argues that many mentally ill people who are not medicated are not competent to make sound choices. He further notes that numerous unmedicated people with schizophrenia end up being homeless and living on the street or being jailed for petty crimes.

Lawyers from the American Civil Liberties Union (ACLU) have argued that forcing the mentally ill to take their medication violates patients' rights.

"The quality of life for homeless individuals with a severe psychiatric illness is a national disgrace," Torrey says. "Studies have found that 28 percent of them get some food from garbage cans and 9 percent use garbage cans as their primary food source. Studies have also shown that at least a third of homeless mentally ill women have been raped. The mortality rate of homeless mentally ill individuals is exceedingly high, including a suicide rate of approximately 15 percent." Torrey and his followers stress that much of this human pain and suffering could be greatly reduced with a daily pill.

Recovering from Schizophrenia

Five

Getting the right medication is crucial for people with schizophrenia. After symptoms are under control, however, patients may still need help in other areas. Mental-health experts have different ideas about what recovery means when dealing with patients with schizophrenia.

Dr. Courtenay M. Harding, a professor of psychiatry at Boston University, defines recovery as reconstituted (fully repaired) social and work behaviors, less dependence on medications, the absence of symptoms, and no need for compensation, or government money given to those unable to work. Harding defines "significant improvement" as

59

"someone who has recovered all but one of those areas [listed above]."

On the other hand, Dr. William A. Anthony, director of Boston University's Center for Psychiatric Rehabilitation, offers a somewhat broader definition of what recovering from schizophrenia means. He sees recovery as "a way of living a satisfying, hopeful, and contributing life even with limitations caused by illness." Anthony added that "recovery doesn't mean a return to a previous level of functioning; it means a more meaningful and purposeful life than one in an institution."

It's difficult to say who is right. At this time, there are no hard-and-fast rules or answers. Experts—as well as patients and their families—simply see the situation differently.

It is generally agreed that, for some people, schizo-phrenia is an illness from which they never fully recover. But do more people actually recover than is known? "The stereotype everyone has of this disease is that there's no such thing as recovery," notes Dr. Torrey. Yet he adds, "The fact is that recovery is more common than people have been led to believe."

Inspiring Success Stories

There are some inspiring success stories. One is that of psychiatrist Daniel B. Fischer, who was hospitalized for schizophrenia three times before he reached the age of thirty. Today, Dr. Fischer is a successful psychiatrist and an advocate for the mentally ill. He has not needed antipsychotic medication in nearly thirty years and has not been hospitalized since 1974.

In describing the factors that went into his recovery, Fischer says, "I'm sure it helped me that I come from a professional family and I was educated. What helped me recover was not drugs, which were one tool I used; it was people. I had a psychiatrist who always believed in me, and family and friends who stood by me. Changing my career [from biochemistry] and following my dream—becoming a doctor—was very important."

The value of a caring environment has been cited in other cases of recovery, as well. Ronald Bassman was diagnosed with schizophrenia as a young man, but his ability to cope with the illness has been remarkable. After earning a doctorate, he became involved in the patient advocate programs of the New York State Office of Health.

"It's remarkable how people come back [from mental illness]," Bassman states. "If you talk to someone who is doing better, he or she will tell you that someone—a friend, a family member, a pastor, a therapist—reached out with warmth and gentleness, and kindness. This is not what is typically done in the mental health system."

Perhaps the best-known case of recovery from schizophrenia is that of the brilliant mathematician and Nobel Prize winner, John Forbes Nash Jr. Nash's story became known to millions with the release of the movie *A Beautiful Mind*, which is loosely based on his life. In the film, as well as in real life, Nash overcame his delusions and was able to return to teaching.

> ### *"I don't think any of us know for sure how many people recover."*
> ### *—Dr. E. Fuller Torrey*

In the movie, Nash's symptoms decline with age, and apparently, this is not uncommon in people with schizophrenia. Some researchers believe that by the time people with schizophrenia reach their mid-forties, the level of chemicals in the brain that may be linked to schizophrenia declines. Therefore, the disease symptoms become less intense. Some patients also learn how to better handle the disease over time.

Such success stories give people hope, but are they the exception to the rule? A number of recent studies seem to suggest that with proper care and a broad range of available rehabilitative services, more people with schizophrenia are doing considerably better than expected. As Torrey states,"I don't think any of us know for sure how many people recover."

Difficulties with Day-to-Day Living

Often people recovering from schizophrenia experience difficulty with communication, self-care, and the establishment of satisfying relationships. Because schizophrenia usually surfaces in early adulthood—during the traditional career-building years—occupational assistance may be necessary.

That was the case for Cameron, a twenty-two-year-old man who had been battling schizophrenia since he was nineteen. He was a freshman in college when the first signs of illness appeared, and things continued to get worse. In and out of mental hospitals, Cameron tried taking different drugs in varying doses.

He eventually began feeling better, but in some ways it was as if his life had stopped when the illness started. "I didn't have a college degree and I didn't feel sure enough of myself to go back to school full time," said Cameron. "I didn't think that I could handle the stress. I felt uncomfortable telling people about my illness so I didn't go out much. The medication had chased away the demons that plagued me but I needed more help. I was spending most days sleeping and watching TV on the couch in my parents' living room."

Treatments are available to help combat the psychological and social problems people with schizophrenia often have. Frequently, these treatments are the next step for people like Cameron once they are on medication.

Some of these treatments include rehabilitation, individual psychotherapy, family education, and self-help groups.

Rehabilitation

Rehabilitation covers a broad range of services for people with schizophrenia. An important phase of rehabilitation is helping the individual acquire the skills necessary to be a productive member of the community. During rehabilitation, many people attend vocational counseling and job training. Trained counselors help these individuals identify their skills and areas of interest. Afterward, individuals may be referred to an educational or job-training center.

Services such as these proved to be just what Cameron needed. He worked with a counselor, who eventually placed him in a program where he learned the basics of computer repair. She also helped him find a part-time job in the field and later helped him enroll in computer courses at the local community college.

Rehabilitation can deal with basic, everyday needs, as well. Patients may be given help with planning a budget, handling savings and checking accounts, shopping, using public transportation, and making new friends. As further explained in the Harvard Mental Health Letter: "Behavioral techniques, including social skills training, are one widely used form of help. Schizophrenic patients are coached, prompted, and corrected as they rehearse behavior and observe others as models. They are shown how to cash checks, prepare for interviews, sustain a conversation, and even clean and dress themselves."

Cigarettes and Schizophrenia

Research indicates that an overwhelming number of people with schizophrenia smoke cigarettes. The studies further show that these individuals tend to be extremely heavy smokers—sometimes smoking as many as several packs a day. It is suspected that the nicotine in cigarettes helps people with schizophrenia to block out environmental distractions that make it harder for them to concentrate. It's also been shown that the nicotine withdrawal that occurs when a person stops smoking often results in a worsening of some of the symptoms of schizophrenia, such as delusions and hallucinations. This may make people with schizophrenia less likely to want to quit smoking.

Individual Psychotherapy

This form of treatment involves regularly scheduled talks (or therapy) with a psychiatrist, psychologist, social worker, or other mental-health professional. During these visits, patients discuss their feelings and how they are handling things. The therapist will assist the patient with his or her problem areas, suggesting better ways to deal with similar situations in the future. Through individual psychotherapy, many patients develop improved coping skills.

Some therapists also work with their patients on critical-thinking skills to help them better deal with the delusions and hallucinations that are common in schizophrenia. In some instances, according to the Harvard Mental Health Letter, therapists try to teach their patients to "evaluate and correct their delusional ideas and hallucinatory perceptions." Therapists urge patients to see that these thoughts and voices have nothing to do with reality. Although this approach to schizophrenia is not always successful, some research shows that it is more effective in helping patients recognize delusions than hallucinations.

Sometimes, patients with schizophrenia also benefit from group-therapy sessions. In these settings, they share their feelings and experiences with a group of people under the supervision of a trained therapist.

Family Education

Families with a member suffering from schizophrenia should learn as much as possible about the disease. This is important because people released from mental hospitals often live, at least temporarily, with their families. Families also need to interact as positively as possible with the affected individual. Often, they can learn how to do so with the help of a social worker or family counselor familiar with the illness.

Family members can play a crucial role in seeing that patients continue to take their medicine and do not miss their doctor appointments. Relatives close to the person with schizophrenia may also be able to tell when relapses start to occur. This puts them in a good position to see that the person quickly gets the necessary help.

Some patients and their families have joined with others in similar situations in demanding more information about available treatment programs and medications. Besides being better informed, they also want more of a say in the kinds of treatment programs offered for the mentally ill. Sometimes referring to themselves as mental-health consumers or survivors, these individuals want their voices heard. One commonly used slogan is "Nothing about us, without us."

Having a family member with schizophrenia can be emotionally draining for relatives, so it is important that counseling services be made available to family members. This is especially important where children are concerned. These young people may not be able to understand what their parent is going through and why their mother or father may seem different. One woman describes what it

"The mother who made me laugh when we watched television together, the mother who listened to music and danced with my friends and me, the mother who combed my hair for school each day, and the mother who made sure I was safe at night did not return home [from the state hospital]."

was like to have a mother with schizophrenia: "[My mother] appeared very different when she returned [from the hospital]. She moved slowly and she had gained weight. Her eyes appeared dazed, her speech was slurred, and at times her hands trembled. I tried extremely hard not to be afraid of her, but I did not know this person who used to be my mother."

Self-Help Groups

In recent years, self-help groups for schizophrenics have become increasingly available. Perhaps the best known is Schizophrenics Anonymous (SA), a self-help group that operates under the sponsorship of the National Schizophrenia Foundation. SA is designed as a support group for people with schizophrenia or related disorders. Members meet to share their feelings and experiences with others who have had to overcome similar obstacles.

A Tool for Self-Help

The purpose of Schizophrenics Anonymous (SA) is:

- *to help restore dignity and a sense of purpose for persons who are working for recovery from schizophrenia or related disorders*
- *to offer fellowship, positive support, and companionship in order to achieve good mental health*
- *to improve members' attitudes about their lives and their illness*
- *to provide members with the latest information regarding schizophrenia*
- *to encourage members to take positive steps toward recovering from the illness*

Joanne Verbanic, who founded SA in 1985, has observed that members who attend meetings regularly tend to do better and feel better. "Our members are able to make important strides toward recovery. Some get jobs, do volunteer work, or go back to school. Others simply begin to participate in the meeting, in what is sometimes their only interaction during the week with people other than their family... People with schizophrenia need a home of their own when it comes to self-help groups."

Schizophrenia is a difficult and complex illness. Researchers are hoping to learn more about its causes as well as find better treatment methods. The National Institute of Mental Health stresses that the outlook for people with schizophrenia has greatly improved over the last twenty-five years and that many people with this illness now lead independent, satisfying lives. It is hoped that many more will do so in the future.

Glossary

abnormality: a condition or feature that is not usually present

advocate: to speak out in favor of or to promote something

agranulocytosis: a serious blood disorder in which there is an insufficient number of white blood cells, or granulocytes

antipsychotics: a group of medications used to control the symptoms of schizophrenia and other disorders

chronic: ongoing or continuing

compensation: the act of making up for

competent: able to handle a particular task

conspiracy: a plot to do something harmful

coping: dealing with or handling something well

delusion: false, often bizarre belief that a person thinks is true

functional magnetic resonance imaging (fMRI): a high-tech scan that provides a picture of the brain's ever-changing activity by tracking the flow of blood to the brain

hallucination: something that a person sees, feels, hears, or smells that isn't there

individual psychotherapy: regularly scheduled talks with a qualified mental-health professional, during which patients discuss their feelings and learn better ways of coping

insomnia: the ongoing problem of being unable to sleep

magnetic resonance imaging (MRI): a high-tech scan that can provide detailed images of the brain's internal structure as well as that of other parts of the body

maintenance treatment: the continued long-term use of medication to control the symptoms of schizophrenia

malnutrition: a state of poor nutrition

monotonous: repetitious or boringly uniform

neuroleptics: antipsychotic drugs developed in the 1950s designed to reduce the symptoms of schizophrenia

neurotransmitter: substance that allows communication between nerve cells in the brain

penal institutions: prisons

predisposing: making something more likely to happen

psychosis: a mental state characterized by hallucinations and delusions

psychotherapy: a form of counseling in which a person examines his or her feelings and explores better ways of coping

relapsing: becoming ill again after a partial recovery

schizophrenia: a severe brain disease in which people lose touch with reality

symptoms: signs of an illness

vocational: related to a job or workplace

Further Resources

Books

Abramowitz, Melissa. *Schizophrenia.* San Diego: Lucent Books, 2002.

Bellenir, Karen. *Mental Health Information for Teens: Health Tips for Teens about Mental Health and Mental Illness.* Detroit: Omnigraphics, 2001.

Camenson, Blythe. *Real People Working in the Helping Professions.* New York: McGraw-Hill, 1997.

Clayton, Lawrence. *Careers in Psychology.* New York: Rosen, 1992.

Demetriades, Helen A. *Bipolar Disorder, Depression, and Other Mood Disorders.* Berkeley Heights, N.J.: Enslow Books, 2002.

Harmon, Daniel E. *Schizophrenia: Losing Touch with Reality.* Broomall, Pa.: Chelsea House, 1999.

Herstek, Amy Paulson. *Dorothea Dix: Crusader for the Mentally Ill.* Berkeley Heights, N.J.: Enslow Books, 2001.

Ketelsen, David P., and Jane E. Phillips. *Schizophrenia.* Berkeley Heights, N.J.: Enslow Books, 2003.

Schleichert, Elizabeth. *The Life of Dorothea Dix.* New York: 21st Century Books, 1991.

Wilkinson, Beth. *Careers Inside the World of Health Care.* Lebanon, Ind.: Globe Fearon Publishers, 1999.

Zucker, Faye. *Depression.* Danbury, Conn.: Children's Press, 2003.

Online Sites and Organizations

The National Alliance for the Mentally Ill (NAMI)
www.nami.org
This Web site provides information on laws affecting the mentally ill as well as other data on living with schizophrenia and other mental illnesses.

National Mental Health Association (NMHA)

www.nmha.org

This Web site represents the nation's oldest and largest nonprofit organization dealing with mental-health issues. It offers information on education, research, and the rights of the mentally ill.

National Mental Health Consumers' Self-Help Clearinghouse

www.mhselfhelp.org

This Web site of a consumer-run national service provides information about the variety of mental-health resources available.

Index

About the Author

Award-winning author **Elaine Landau** received a bachelor's degree in English and journalism from New York University and a master's degree in library and information science from Pratt Institute. She worked as a newspaper reporter, children's book editor, and a youth services librarian before becoming a full-time writer. She has written more than two hundred nonfiction books for children and young adults. She lives in Miami, Florida, with her husband, Norman, and their son, Michael.